The Book of the Rotten Daughter

Poetry by Alice Friman

Books

Zoo
Inverted Fire
Reporting from Corinth

Chapbooks

Driving for Jimmy Wonderland
Insomniac Heart
Song to My Sister
A Question of Innocence

The Book of the Rotten Daughter

Alice Friman

BkMk Press
University of Missouri-Kansas City

BkMk Press
University of Missouri-Kansas City
5101 Rockhill Road
Kansas City, Missouri 64110
(816) 235-2558 (voice)
(816) 235-2611 (fax)
bkmk@umkc.edu
http://www.umkc.edu/bkmk

MAC
MISSOURI ARTS COUNCIL

Financial support for this project has been provided by the Missouri
Arts Council, a state agency.

Book design: Adriana Arteaga & Susan L. Schurman
Cover photographs: Lillian Elaine Wilson
Managing Editor: Ben Furnish
Associate Editor: Michelle Boisseau
Printing: Walsworth Publishing Company, Marceline, Missouri

BkMk wishes to thank:
Bill Beeson, Heather Clark, Jennifer Echavarria, Christopher Glenn,
Kate Melles, Michael Nelson, David E. Rowe.

Library of Congress Cataloging-in-Publication Data
Friman, Alice.
  The book of the rotten daughter / by Alice Friman.
    p. cm.
  Summary: "*The Book of the Rotten Daughter* offers poems from
Alice Friman's experience as care-giver for her aging mother and
father, exploring such topics as nursing homes, osteoporosis,
guilt, grief, the enduring power of familial relationships, and the
transcendent power of art"—Provided by publisher.
  PS3556.R5685B66   2006
  811'.54—dc22

                              2005031760

This book is set in Josephine, Lucida Grande and Lucida Bright type.

To my mother and to my father
and to my sister, who was there

Acknowledgments

The author wishes to thank the editors of the following journals and anthologies where the poems in this volume first appeared:

Boulevard: "Visitation Rights," "Sunday's Gift," "From the Daughter Journals," "Letter to My Sister," "Visiting Robinson"

Field: "The Fall," "Lost in Space," "Shattering," "The Dream of the Rotten Daughter"

The Georgia Review: "Snow," "Drought"

The Gettysburg Review: "Preparatory Meditations," "The Wish"

Image: "Seymour's Last Ride"

The Malahat Review (Canada): "Ghost Story for December," "Sonic Boom," "The Sound," "Osteoporosis"

Margie: "Dressing the Skeleton," "Eyesore"

New Letters: "After Shooting the Barbados Ram," "Footnote"

North American Review: "At the Holocaust Museum"

North Dakota Quarterly: "The Gulf"

The Ohio Review: "Final Instructions," "In an Angry Vein," "The Vigil," "This April," "The Condensed Version"

Prairie Schooner: "Sub Rosa," "Remembering in Lilac and Heart-Shaped Leaves," "Tribute"

Shenandoah: "Otma Rood"

The Southern Review: "Dust"

Witness: "The Talent Show"

The Worcester Review: "Dallas"

"The Empty Garden" was published in *Falling Toward Grace*, Indiana University Press and The Polis Center. "At the Holocaust Museum" was also published in *The Winners of the Miriam Lindberg Israel Poetry for Peace Prize* (Israel) and *Voices Israel.* "Otma Rood" won the 2002 James Boatwright III Prize for Poetry from *Shenandoah.*

The author is grateful to The MacDowell Colony, The Virginia Center for the Creative Arts, and the Mary Anderson Center, where many of these poems were written. The author also wishes to thank all good friends who have helped over the years with encouragement, advice, and endurance, especially Roger Pfingston, Bill Trowbridge, Jenny Kander, Marilyn Kallet, Fran Quinn, and my husband, Bruce Gentry. I am also deeply indebted and grateful to Dale Kushner for her abiding friendship, her insights, and the inspiration of her own writing.

The writing of these poems was aided by a fellowship from the Indiana Arts Commission and a Creative Renewal Fellowship from the Arts Council of Indianapolis.

Contents

I

II

III

The Dream of the Rotten Daughter

On the night of the day
she buried her mother

her father turned to her
from the grip of an old

photograph, her six-year
dead daddy, swiveled his

bullet head, nailing her
to him with a bloodshot

sniggery eye, then stuck
out his tongue. She woke up

laughing, recognizing
the title of this book

before she wrote it, there
on the point of that red

wad where he'd honed it all
those years, slipping it in

between her ribs when she
least expected. It was

his label for her from
the time of the big bed

Sunday mornings, and she
between them pretending

oblivion, a balled-
up cuddle to bridge their

unbridgeable gap. Or
(speak truth, oh rotten one)

usurp the I'm-here-first
of that furious eye.

Old news, old news. Tell it
another way. Make it

a Halloween story,
Poe story—ghouls, spiders,

cellars and foul air. Two
dolls in their boxes, laid

side by side like people
bewitched in an iron sleep

and a ghost with a blood
eye and a butcher's tongue

who cut his way into
his daughter's dream to say

of the newly dead, *Boo!*
I won. I've got her now.

AFTER SHOOTING THE BARBADOS RAM

Because his neighbor's boy wanted the horns
he whacked off the top of the head
straight across
leaving the brain in the grass—
two tablespoons of squiggle
and the brain pan
lined in ivory, empty except for the flies.

I watch because I must,
not because my grinning brother-in-law
waving his bloody knife
shoves the scene in my face—the ram
strung up by the hind legs
then slit down the middle, the insides
tumbling out into a tub. The one
undescended testicle, knuckle big
and hard as love,
flushed from its hiding place at last.
The body, the hide, adding up to nothing
but a magician's coat emptied of its tricks.
Any two-bit fly buzzy in emerald
is more than this.

But it's the brain I come back to,
separated from the white fibrous fingers
that cradled it, suspended it
easy in a jelly. The Dura Mater.
The enduring mother, holding—
idiot or saint—whatever she's got.
Mama the dependable, tough as bungee straps
or a stevedore's net, hanging on
to her freight until the final dock.

I kneel in the grass,
run my fingers over the brain's empty casing,

think of my father, gone not even a month.
A meningioma, they said. A thickening
of the outer lining. The Dura Mater.
The tough mother who never quits—
who quit. Took up weaving in her boredom,
knitting her own cells into a pile of pillows
then turned, the way milk turns,
the way any mother left alone in the dark
might turn, a pillow in her hands.

They said it was slow growing, decades maybe,
but now, having reached the pons, the bulb
at the base of the brain—.
Look, they said, how the brain struggles
in a narrowed, pinched-in space, rummages
for what it can no longer remember:
the old triggers fired off easy as pop-guns
for ninety years—pump, pump, breathe.

I kneel over the ram's motherless brain
the way I bent over him, holding the hand
that for sixty-two years refused mine,
singing the song he never sang for me.
The crusted mouth. The lolling tongue.
The eyes unable to close
because the brain had forgotten how.
The breath still so sweet.

DROUGHT

The trees rattle their discontent,
cheated out of the juice of summer.
They will shut down early,
pitch their trashy leaves
and board up. One young beech
aborted already, ditching her progeny
as dried mistakes. The old ones
know better, concentrate on roots.
Underground, blind as moles, an army
of hairy tips creeps toward the lake.
Ah, but the lake too is thirsty.
See how cleverly it tucks itself
under the lily pads to lap their bottoms,
knowing safety lies in the shadow
of their contentment where it hides,
guzzling itself down.

Sixty-five days of this.
Sixty-five with no end in sight.
The forest so dry, each bug or bird
gives itself away with rustling
and all mystery equals the daily news.
Even the creek bed, all along
its lovely length, has forgotten
the sweet weight of water, its lull
and churn—the boulder's wet dream
of hard rain, of swollen rush
and black slide over the top
all thrust and glitter and drown.
Under the bottom shale no damp,
no dirt is left to remember. Only sand
whispering down then deeper down
granule to granule to granule. *Thirst.*

I think of the tyger Billy Blake

banged out, the face he knew he'd see
in the mirror of that cat's eye.
So I know, standing knee-deep
in this disaster that used to be meadow,
that I too am parched
and straw-minded as this meadow
scraping and scratching at its itch.
Sixty-five years of this.
Sixty-five with no end before the end
in sight. Boiled down to an angry bone
knocking in a soup of dried grasses
stirred by the hot clang of a wind.
What were once wildflowers—purples
and doilies and blazing stars—reduced
to cinders, dried black and stuck on stems.

THIS APRIL

I follow a pig truck
down I-65 redolent with spring.
Truckers roll their winter sleeves.
Dandelions mug from the berm.
Only the trees hold out, arms up
full of waiting. Not one green blush
among them. Still, they must know,
swaying like sisters gathered in a kitchen
remembering the dance.

I head south to the woods
ten miles north of the Ohio River
to walk where I walked in a bad December,
leading my footprints down to the lake,
sending my breath like icy ghosts
into the brush looking for my mother.

Today I return, looking for myself,
hoping, if nothing else, my shoes
will find me, divining in dirt
for the soles' zigzags, last seen
wandering in snow, repeating themselves
like first sounds over and over, mama mama.

LOST IN SPACE

from a sculpture by Henry Moore

How turned in
these women are, complete
in their big bronze lives.
Even the reclining one, knob for head
and no delineations—no nose,
no nipples, no sunshine slot. No limbs
reaching from the body, no wild music
pinging in her thigh. Nothing but a hole
big as a fist drilled through her chest.
Yet how complacent, ho-hum she is
about that gap being there, surrounded by
a flesh polished to a bronze Pacific
that can't remember a time the hole
was ever filled, with fire maybe or gristle
or a daisy, simple as a heart.

Today the museum is filled
with mistakes. Even the information plaques
are wrong. Euterpe for Terpsichore.
One muse taken for the other.
The one who danced, lost
like the dance itself, fallen through
and forgotten, there being no plug,
no thumb in the dike big enough to hold it.

It's easy to play bloodhound
when something is left—a dirty sock,
two sneakers kicked off under a desk,
a whiff of pencil shavings, and the child
is home once more doing her algebra
before the telephone call
and the calendar page never to be turned again.

But a hole with no stopper
is a tub of everything that matters
running out, a perpetual wash of thoroughness.
The grand design of flush and swirl.
Might as well tickle a dead body
as ask a woman with a lobotomy in her chest
to remember where the dazzle went
or the lost dance in which to find it.

SNOW

Let us speak of love and weather
subtracting nothing.
Let us put your mother and mine
away for a while. Your dying father,
my dead one.
                    Let us watch
from our bedroom window how a slow
falling snow crowns all nakedness in ermine.
Do not look at me yet. Your face is flushed,
your eyes too love-soaked, too blue.
Outside is white on black
and still. The sky, deaf with stillness.

Don't let it frighten you.
Hush. There's time enough for that.
Be content for now to watch the maples
fill with snow, how they spread themselves,
each naked limb making itself accessible.

Remembering in Lilac and Heart-Shaped Leaves

See how they've laid out the lilacs.
A parade—seven rows across,
sixteen down. And I who never
cared much for spring, the pasteled chirp
and buzz of it, lose myself among them—
tuba in the flutes, nettle in the iris bed.
It isn't the scent, though they beat out
last month's hyacinths guaranteed to stink up
a whole house despite their famous hair.

Look, my middle name's not Joy.
It's Ruth, named for the stranger
sniffling and nose-blowing her way
across wilderness, following the scuff
of a mother-in-law's shoe. Ruth the Moabite,
the Blotter, the Good, programmed
to soak up sorrow the way an unlit match
is programmed to absorb the dark.

You know this story—
how she stood, lightning rod
in the fields of luck where everyone knows
rich equals handsome equals virtuous.
And if Boaz turned out Palooka
who scratched his parts and wore his
money belt to bed, who bibbled over dinner
about goats and the price of barley,
who eyed her bodice while he grouched
of fallow fields and picked his ear,
who wants to know?

It's beginnings we want. Act I.
Curtain up, and there she is
standing amid Keats's *alien corn*—woman

on the threshold, Rachel at the well,
Cinderella before the ball or Juliet after,
trembling toward sacrifice. How we want

to keep them in that moon's first spotlight—
Ruth's straight back, Juliet's hand to cheek
in gesture and cue with Romeo the nail-biter
swoony behind lilacs—the night air
staggering beneath the weight
of all their untaken breaths.

OTMA ROOD

Shackled to that name, by fifteen
she knew the rest the stars dished out
would stack up equal: a mother-in-law
who cooked forty years for the railroad,
raising eight perfect kids to boot. And Joe,
shot dead in the grocery that Friday night
late August, figuring receipts.

Go to Ten Mile Creek. Look there
for what she was, mud-trailing skirts
in her daily crash through woods,
racketing trees with a peeled stick,
mouthing the words she chewed on each day
of her life to suck the bitter out—same as
the creek hid under its breath, lugging rain
to the long brown thirst of the Arkansas.
Even Joe—sweeping, marking tins—knew
how poetry can settle young on a girl
who labeled herself cashed-in ugly
each time she had to write a check.

Take the turnpike east out of Tyler
where Ten Mile still runs cold
past Kissy Rock, then follow on foot
to where it eddies and stalls, twisting
back on itself to lap at the roots
of the giant sycamore, sucking out
the footings, the underpinnings,
not stopping until the whole white body
drops into its mouth at last. Do you see
how the tree leans back and away, pulling
at its roots the way a woman would
who recognizes the unlucky label
of her name on the underside of love

and knows she has to get away, but can't?

Here Otma Rood must have walked
and stopped to lean. And maybe it was here
she saw it. A bird? Who can tell.
A dive of color then a swoop. Or make
it night, late August, when the wild sky,
risking theft, unhinges all its fire.
And she, widow now and womb pregnant
with the only shot at freedom
she would ever have to give a name to—

Juanita. Proxy. Shooting star.

THE WISH

This is a story for the ends of August
when the days yawn
and roll over, the hot nights
dragging their insomnia of stars,
when the lake's lily pads,
so shoulder-shoving thick you're
sure you could walk them, spin
on sky water—Chinese dinner plates
floating on sticks—twirling so fast
you'd swear they're not moving.

This is the tale of a pharmacist's wife
who at the age of forty
bobbed her nose, fluffed herself up,
and waited for the cards to deliver.
VISA, MasterCard, Discover—
she was ready. Her hippie hairdresser,
the TV repairman, the piano tuner.
And when the fates turned up the yeshiva boy
with black hair, red eyes and allergies,
she bought him a gold necklace, dubbed him
Prince of the Aztecs, and deflowered him
in the wildflowers of the field.

What else did she know to do,
brought up on Hollywood
and married to a pharmacist who couldn't
fill her prescription? That summer,
staring out their night window while he
counted pill bottles in his sleep,
she made her wish, her deal—
all or nothing. And when Nothing
turned up—the gutterball,
the short straw, the King of Spades

masquerading as oncologist—
she took Him too, stiff
as a ball peen hammer between
her legs, stiff as a sentence
and as insistent. Mr. Nothing, the only one
true-blue enough to know how to love her,
starting with one breast then the other,
taking His good sweet time,
not missing a lick until she was through.

SONIC BOOM

Last week my husband found out
the lump in his neck was a wait
and we'll watch it, keep track of
on a chart. Adam's apple's
younger brother, Pip the Bomb—

defused for now but still
all-day fiddled with
like a pet hangnail
or the good-luck aggie
parked with his pocket junk
nightly on the dresser—notes,
keys, paper clips. The change.

This is hard.
I come from a family of Russians
stubborn as stumps. Crabby, but we live.
He's sunny with a history.
Aunts, uncles, cousins—in
out the revolving door.

Another morning. NPR
and pink grapefruit on a plate.
A bridge of silence between us.
What's to say? We need words
between vitamin C and the granola,
a suspension of *now*, a drawbridge
to lift and stop the mental traffic,
lift and let back in, bright
on blue water, our Italian summer:

The attic room in Palermo. A window
big as a Murphy bed opening into the sky
and how daisy in skin we were

floating beneath on fields of sheet,
all white cotton. The sky ballooning
into a blue hotel of hours—
a vast book or a mind
where swallows arced and scooped
criss-crossing our names. What's to say
except repeat the forever we were that day
before the sky broke and frightened all the birds.

SHATTERING

1.
Tonight in your arms
watching over your sleep,
unable for three nights now
to let go of you, I imagine
(can't help but imagine) you
on that high floor
calling to say *Love*
as if I didn't know that
already, but you, like so
many others, needing to
lay down that
as your last word,
terrified you'll not get out
before that too tall building
slides down its sides
although you couldn't have
known that then, could you,
there being only the weight
of that fire coming at you
and you so afraid.
                    And I know
because I love you, I'd have
to talk you out of there,
making my voice the fireman's
ladder, the helicopter's rope
that never came. Come, my own,
my blue-eyed boy, I'd say,
walk out on the running nap
of my voice, my voice
your carpet, your cocoon,
your velvet corridor out.
But the fire, the fire. Shhh.
Seal the lids to your eyes.

Nothing is but where I'm waiting.
And Now Love, Now—for now
there must be nothing
but us between us. And simple
as placing one foot after another,
you'd step through a blossom of glass
into the bright blue air.

2.
Is this not crazy?
You're asleep. The plosives
punctuating your breath
poof out your lips like
pudding in a pot or an engine
idling on kisses. While I,
ear to your chest and counting,
borrow scenarios from our latest
terror, as if we didn't have enough
to go around.

                And shame. Look how
self-controlled I made myself,
how Hedda Gablerish, talking
you through such brave
and lovely death, all in the name
of love as if love were a name
without presence or heat,
without a face to xerox
and paste up all over town
or hug to your chest before
the whole world because it was
your heart leaped from your body,
lost and looking for itself.

And again I'm there—
only this time holding up
that photograph of you I love

leaning against the railing
in your blue suit when it was new,
and smiling as if the sun itself
summered in your face. And I—
one more soldier in misery's army
wandering the streets
begging to be listened to:

The fire, the fire. And how
I made of my voice a rug,
a flying carpet to get him out.
And yes, he came to me, yes.
I'm sure. Didn't you see him
running down those staircases of air?

VISITATION RIGHTS

I sit by a ravine dumped with November,
every leaf the color of old pennies. Gingko,
oak, maple, hackberry—no difference.
Back to the dirt factory.

Why isn't that comfort comfort enough?
After all, one makes do: a sycamore
preens in a rag of winter sun and
each mica-studded boulder flinging light away
balls up and waits for heat. Still,
April's promise is midget, parsley on a plate,
compared to this:

High noon and no shadow. December's black-
white, bone-bark schematic
that snow, like Noah's sheet, rushes in to cover,
pretending the sinkhole's not there
or the fallen sparrow broken in a ditch. Look.

The sun's out hunting for his children.
A once-a-week father in a blue car.
A regular Mr. Razzledazzle flashing his brights
on every lake, every puddle, every teaspoon of water
searching for the bodies. *Too late too late*
says my cup of tea. *All the honey's gone.*

GHOST STORY FOR DECEMBER

*Would it be any comfort to know the dead we love
are looking out from behind thick glass at us*
—Eamon Grennan

In Virginia, snow lasts two days
then melts, leaving doilies on lawns
and lumps of swan on the berm.

A woman shivers in a yellow parka
carrying her gloves. She walks
looking for signs of her father,
last reported not moving
and aloof in his satin cupboard
waiting for seepage. She needs
to know he'll stay there
through spring rain and the root
inching a rope toward his heart.

Already she's heard the first fly
of next year buzzing her pane, notes
in her journal how grass in Virginia
gets a head start, holding its green
through winter. She worries
what a twitch of warmth can budge
deep in the sift of soil. And if here
spring comes early, what does it mean
for the father buried in Florida
where hibiscus and heliotrope
and red passionflower
lush as pain keep coming coming
as if there were no such thing as death?

Cave hic poetae. Beware of poets
who play with the dead. It's no comfort
to know her father watches

from behind glass. Or rises
to the surface of a lake—dead fish—
repeating her old name *rotten daughter*
rotten daughter through his mouth hole.

The father she wanted was given,
five days before the end. And that
in the form of a baby whose last breath
settled the lid on a gift. Don't open it.

THE VIGIL

The week my father lay dying
means Florida, high tide and June
waking into her heat. Five nights,
and a swollen moon paces the tide lines
waiting for the brain tumor to finish him,
bulge to the limits of a cold circumference
as if taking instruction all these years
through the pupils of his eyes.

Little old Daddy lost in a bed.
So tired. Even his rage is worn out.

The nurse asks my help, me
the Oedipus xerox, or is it Elektra,
loving a father who delivered nothing
but a crate of sorrows. We turn him,
lift his hips, change his diaper.
The shock-white skin of the redhead.
The milky worm of my making
asleep in its thinned-out thatch.

Mother looks down, at once enamored
with her lap—the separate lives
of her fingers. Their St. Vitus' dance.
Their terrible rummage in her purse.

In a hundred years, ask me.
I'll remember: his five-day
tunnel of sleep rattling toward Friday,
each breath gasping through the ratchet.
Then the business of it. How shadows
outside the window suddenly skidded
then halted in their lengthening

as if every clock in the world had stopped.
And when She came—Lady of Timetables,
Lady of Iron Gates—I knew Mother and I
had nothing more to do with it.

She wrapped him in Her yellow blanket,
humming a tune only he could hear
(a buzz of sugar from the old days)
Charlie Barnett or Guy Lombardo
the sweetest music this side of heaven.
And slowly his right hand—as if
pulled by a balloon on a string—lifted,
the hand of the D– student he always was,
rising in slow motion to the only answer
he ever knew. He stared, the eyes blank
as the moonstone in the silver ring
he wore for fifty years, the stone
the same no-color as Her eyes.

THE SOUND

Since your death
I remember you as I've written
not how you were. The old forgiveness
of child hand in yours comes through
the pen.

Dandelions dot these woods,
violet, bellwort, little pink things.
Last year's death safely underfoot.
Another spring. Another urge
to reinvent.

But even in April—
the forest rinsed in sun
and empty as a waiting jar—I panic
at certain sounds. Not the woodpecker
typing in his high office

or the rotten limb
banging on her dead mother for heat.
But finer: jitters of birds or
last year's dead leaf still rattling
its umbilical twig.

A dogwood
proselytizes in pink, holds up
his crosses—witness, prophet,
Lazarus of the Snows. But look—
here on the path

two dead moles.
And deer, a double trail
ending suddenly. Their final prints
dug in as if stabbed by a sound

they stiffened

in moonlight,
and rigid as two boards
were hauled like spare scenery, up
through slots in air. Old Wound—
was it you?

LETTER TO MY SISTER

To speak of panic in a quiet time
means yelling *fire* in a crowded hall,
wolf in the cottage lane. So I write
to tell you how Mother has settled well
in her new home—room, that is—relieved
there are nurses and their bustlings
to hold her. She's even stopped
grappling at my throat for a while,
twisting the old knives in their holes.
She gains weight, ounce by quarter ounce,
and breath comes easier in her chest.

Yesterday at dusk, because I could,
I walked the fields again. Suddenly, deer.
Five white-tails from out of nowhere
come, I imagine, for the last few apples
under the abandoned trees. And I remember
my first shock of elephants in Kenya,
how they too materialized from shadow
or were reborn into it each dusk
like creatures darkness is loath to part with
and so marks—the way water marks
what it once held and loved—
with a wrinkled skin.

And I thought of Mother, shriveling
in her chair. How the wrinkled knuckle-
skin—the seal, stamp, signature
of first water, the birthmark, the return
ticket punched and promised that we carry
with us all life long—has spread,
weaving its net, laying claim.

Enough. As I said, things go well,

although lately she seems to want
the room darkened the way Daddy did.
Remember how his drawn blinds at 4 o'clock
drove her crazy? *Living in a tomb* she'd say
then pull the ropes. The tug of war
goes on between them. It's his turn now.
All their child games: the lines
that connect the dots. *Tap tap, you're it.*
Last line on a box closes it up. It's yours.
You get to put your name on it.

OSTEOPOROSIS

This time around
was to forego cause
and go directly to effect. This time
there was no fall. No P. T. Barnum
of siren and ambulance, only the one-act
spine—that acrobatic clone of brothers
balanced on each other's shoulders
for ninety-two years, until deep
in their marrow minds they felt the crunch
and grind of a slow-motion buckling
and cried *enough.*

(There's variety
in the way people sit.
The stairstep of knee and hip to
accommodate a chair holds secrets
that run along the lifeline of the bone
and burrow in, even with calcium. A girl
milks her secrets, washes them down
with milk, floats them on its white tide
to be deposited like royal mummies
in the catacombs of bone. Who knows
the hour of their waking, the sovereign
greed of their hunger, the irresistible teat
of a sweet bone house?)

All her life
she was ammunition
in a girdle. Pluck and determination
to defeat the ugly—box, bury it
even from herself. Armored in apron,
by Perpetual Order of Stocking and Garter,
she jousted under the big bed,
stabbing with her mop. What dragon

demanded a daily slaying? What permanent
wave of snakes rose from her mirror's
polished shield? What secret
thinned to a fault line in the bone
betrays her now? Crumple of paper
lost in a bed. Breaker of my heart.

The Talent Show

Easing herself up on her walker,
she shuffled into the cleared space.
It was "Back Home Again in Indiana"
and maybe because she'd had it up to here
with being tractable
or that the singing part of her knew
not every note had landed in the right place,
Bertha G. sang it again and then again
until *the new mown hay in all its fragrance*
quivered into its ricks. And everyone clapped.

Next, Rose (of the hair ribbon to match) rose
and, trembling in the old way of patriotism,
unleashed "The Star-Spangled Banner"
only to lose it in the high reaches of rockets
and red glare. Then Joe, practicing his tune
all morning on the clarinet, disappeared,
sending Social Services scouring the halls
in a fluster to find him while the aides
whooped and lined themselves up swinging
to the beat of The Cha-Cha Slide, stomped
and shook their booties. And everyone said
the day was Big Success. Better than Bingo
or the time Jungle Bob—with the snakes
and turtle that never came out of its shell—
dragged in the dog, trained to whimper and
lay his head in everyone's lap, and they all
petted it because they were told except Mother
who wanted no part of it.
                    Then hooray—
ice cream in cups and cupcakes with sprinkles.
And everyone unwrapped their own wooden spoon
except Armine Bonner, 116B,
who'll not let go of her dolly for anything.

Two years ago Mother would have said
the whole thing was hokey. America's old—
the new adorables. The *alte cuties.*
But I have faith. I watched Armine Bonner
pinch her baby with her left hand so
she'd have something to comfort with her right.
And Bertha's still singing her Indiana song
up and down the corridors while the red balloon
tied to her walker bobbles over her head
like bloody sunshine or a trophy for roaring.

In an Angry Vein

Last night, I dreamed again—
adult potty chairs and corridors,
cottage cheese and peaches on a tray.
Nothing that shines. Not even language
to pull me out and awake. No metaphor
to wrap my new life in, only a jumble
of paraphernalia and the red button
she pushes and pushes for no one to come.

Yesterday I did her nails,
held each trembling finger to file
and swab, cream with Intensive Care.
The veins bulging across each ache
and knob, down each arthritic knuckle,
weaving a net to hold them. Poor veins.
Mama's veins. Tote bag for bones.
Each cord, bruise-blue and swollen
as a traffic jam or a telephone wire
clogged with voices desperate to get out.

We play a game of cassino. She naps, stirs,
asks again when dinner's served
and where. I push her in her chair,
earning my ticket (my sister says) to heaven.
My sister's wrong.

A little girl holds her breath
for ninety years. The veins labor,
wrestle with their knots. A story, a story.
Little girl needs to dredge up the story.
And I, for the life of me, don't have the heart
to make her ream it out.

THE FALL

The carpet tilted like the sea.
And she who never walked on water
tipped, spun, then toppled—

a bundle of sticks,
Pinocchio's old mother
come apart in her strings.

The way I watched
you'd think it was Channel 8,
another trick at the Olympics—

another triple lutz gone wrong,
except she didn't get up
to do it again, smiling stupid

for the judges. No judges.
Only me in the mirror, ticking off
in a ledger how once again

I failed to rescue her in time
the way she taught me,
the way she always taught me

how to love her love her,
little girl imperious or flailing
arthritic in my arms.

Now she sits in a chair.
The slinged arm prophetic as albatross,
heavy as the cast of her 91 years

hanging from both our necks—
her Purple Heart, her Olympic gold.

My alloy dipped in gilt.

Funny how things break down,
like when wires cross in the phone
and the conversation you bargained for—

the one life you sunned
and watered like a petunia—
splits into two.

Today we share an orange.
I strip it with my nail. The navel,
a hard wet knot under the skin.

Old Gray Bird—please,
today let's embrace the augury
of peel, fallen unbroken to the dish.

No more bulletins from the interior,
the study of entrails, the ominous
bawk bawk of the failed bowel.

I know I know: the fall
that will end it—hip or spine.
Any day now you remind me.

Mother, not to worry.
The short straw you've longed for
is in your hand at last.

One day you will succeed.
I have a talent for failure.
I've been practicing all my life.

The Empty Garden

Hooverwood Nursing Home, 1997

In the Myth of the Garden
was the beginning,
the pulse
that pulls us all life long

back to the fountain,
the apple trees, the beds
of wild silence.
What difference the day?

Sabbath crowns *every* morning,
eases the shades at night.
But there *is* no return.
I wish I could tell you

different: how in this
nursing home, the oldest
of old who've lived so long
and are so close

are pulled to this garden
where they wait, huddled
in afghans,
clutching teddy or doll,

and tip their faces to the sun.
Or sit by the window
taking delight
in the progress of spring,

schooling themselves on bulbs—
their green tongues, the pink
or yellow kiss

of a one-shot flower.

Or this: how each dawn
before the nurses unlatch
and lower the bed rails, an army
of the bent and trembling,

the arthritic, the feeble
and forgetful, rise
like crumples of paper
from their beds—your mother

and mine—stooped
and tottering histories
in slippersocks and flannel,
and hanging on furniture

work a path to the window
for that first clean blade of light
that's hacked its way
through blinds to find them.

If only, if only.
Then I too could believe
in an almost-angel mother
knocking on window glass

to her friend, the only
face she recognizes—
the other cloudy wonder
across the courtyard—and she

waving back, nodding *yes yes*
and pointing—
this daffodil or that
as if this day at least

she understood *clap*
your hands and sing. Spring
is back and waiting for us
in the garden. Sassy

and hopeful
as a yellow school bus
opening and closing its wheezy door
then out the gates at last.

From the Daughter Journals

As whales plow through krill,
swifts stream out of their chimney

gleaning a bug breakfast from the air.
An old cardinal knocks a young one

off his wire. A gang of crows swoops in
looking for a morning argument. I sit

by the lake, watching how trees lean
diagonal, tending to their reflections,

wondering if they too are joined—stuck
root to root—as if those look-alikes

towering in the fretful water,
those dead ringers, were their mothers.

By December each leaf loss will be
set down in the surface records

revealing the skeletons of an ancient
tug of war: the arcing up / the lodestone

down. The stretch of bare-boned cracking,
the drag of deaf and trembling water.

What's this of whales and krill?
Here is my center post. Here

where the toad freezes and stares,
and the old oak hangs on to her leaves

all winter, running a nursing home for

her children death-rattling in her arms.

Oh Mother, forgive me.
I have bad dreams. Everything

seems to know my name, writes me
into its daily movie. I can't seem

to go more gently into your good night.
I'm afraid you are taking me with you.

DRESSING THE SKELETON

If your specimen
isn't the medical school variety—
suspended from a hook or neck-locked
in a standing position—you'll find
placing it seated in a padded chair
works best. Without the supportive
structures of tendon, ligaments, etc.,
maintaining a good vertical balance
long enough to complete the procedure
can be tricky, if not impossible.

Start with the panties.
Taking one foot at a time, cradle
the bones in one hand while you slip
the elastic over the medial arch. Slacks
go on much the same way, except in order to
get each foot through in one smooth motion
you'll have to bunch up the cloth
which will result in a twist of pants
and underpants suspended between the tarsals
and synovial joint of the knee. I find
if you seat yourself facing the project
and hook the hand and finger phalanges
to your shoulders, then gently lift
the entire axial structure to a standing
position, balance can be sustained
for the two or three seconds it will take
to get the layers up, the elastic adjusted.

Dressing the top half should not impose
too many difficulties. Turtle-neck shirts,
especially those with small head openings,
might prove problematic if the cervical
vertebrae can no longer support the weight

of the cranium. Bright colors are preferred.
Oh, yes—make sure to place a thick pad
in the underpants in case the whole thing leaks
or you'll have to start again from scratch.

With mine, I like to finish
with a touch of moisturizing lipstick
before I brush out the hair, still lush
and growing as if it didn't know
the mind had blown its case and it was time to stop.

FOOTNOTE

Maybe after,
from your bed of "ease at last"

you'll give your child
a something. A tap-tap

tapped by your own hand.
A message, by fair or foul means,

sneaked out through your wrap-
around of roots. And I, eyes up

and straining
under that nipple-rooting tree

the way others stood
under the sacred oak in Dodona,

god-drunk on leaves grown fat
on rain, taken in easy

as mother's milk.
But what exorcist, deliverer

of comfort, dare translate for me
when from your tongue

of sullen silence
perfected in the grave

there comes
a heave of earth, a groan

of roots dragging themselves out,
the branches

huddled inside their writhing
sleeves of gibberish: the leaves

gone mad
with your struggle not to say,

not to tell your child,
pure and simple, she was good enough.

III

The Book of the
Rotten Daughter
The Book of the
Rotten Daughter
The Book of the
Rotten Daughter

Final Instructions

When I die I want to be buried
with sweet potatoes candied or
sautéed with apples & cinnamon
or a pile of mashed on a plate
with drumstick or chop & don't
forget sweet & sour with short
ribs & plums in an all-day pot
like Grandma made to be dug up
like Pharaoh wrapped & radiant
in a case & may the burial man
dressed in black whose sad job
means a sour face hoho & whoop
garnishing my body with slices
of yam like Rye Crisp around a
cheese & may he go home & tell
his wife how he pressed one in
each hand & filled my navel up
with a dollop my mouth smeared
in purée & please it should be
October anniversary of the day
I first came stumbling through
the door of an afflicted house
& stayed being I was lost & no
one to ask how to get me found
So Honey heap me a cairn—yams
instead of stones & dump it on
top of me with fanfare & grave
ceremony so I hear it rumbling
like apples in autumn tumbling
in a bin & recognize who I was
In Hawaii they said yam is Fat
Moon's child—pilau—sweetness
from the moon that's what I am
you are—yellow buttons Mama's
buttons ready to slide through
Earth's dirt shirt & button us
to her never to be lost again—

DALLAS

1.
Home from Texas a week
and the sky still sagging, sodden
as a throwaway mattress left at the curb.
By rights the clouds should settle in
northeast of here over Klanville, Indiana,
where they've got the sheets to fit.

But what's all this got to do
with Texas and a city built to look good
from the highway? One concrete monolith
trimmed in day-glow green. And towers
of erection glass rising from the flat belly
of the plains like the Sons of Silicon,
but standing apart, keeping a distance
as if shouldering together for a skyline
would belie their history. Like when
the news got out about Texas: land of
land deals and white guys only. So they came.
Bowie the slave smuggler out of Louisiana
packing a steel-edged hangover. Young Travis
from Alabama, running away from a murder
and letting a black man hang for it.
And Old Man Crockett, the politician, down
in the opinion polls already, with twelve
Tennessee boys who hadn't changed underwear
in a year, hot-eyed kids and hustlers
not knowing all they were doing
was trying out for the John Wayne part,
too big for life but riding the range again—
kingpins of parking lots and blowing papers
and not a soul in sight.

2.

There are no more books
in the Texas Book Depository on the corner
of Elm and Houston. No sign of Dick and Jane
or Little Sally, pigeon-toed in Mary Janes,
or Mother, aproned for life,
except for the display of Scott Foresman cartons
in the corner by the sixth-floor window
where they said he stashed the carbine
made in Italy, serial #2766, a real
bargain—$21.45 through the U.S. mails—
then, hurtling down the steps four at a time,
bought a Coke, fooled a cop,
hit the sidewalk and ran. You remember—
that day of the pink suit, the pillbox hat.

Eight days ago I stood where he stood.
The window so big you could swan dive
into that day again—open car, everyone waving.
America, young enough to break out in pimples.
Another *High Noon* it was. Another Hollywood
once upon a time—Camelot's King Arthur
and the Lone Star playing Russian roulette
at the round table. The skyscrapers
standing around like extras at Ruby's place,
slit-eyed in mirrored glasses, waiting
and apart, as if they had nothing to do with it.

At the Holocaust Museum
December 1999

Like Dante, we too are led
down. The elevator that swooped us up
and spewed us out, leaves us—
clusters of strangers—to the inexorable power
of no way to go but with each other
and the relentless spiral of design.

We shuffle, slow as sludge
in a drain, winding to the bottom.
We gawk, not in disbelief but believing
this has little to do with us—our comfort
in the face of explanations that explain
nothing, the old jackboot footage
of rantings, book burnings, and the car
that waits for us, rattling with ghosts
on its siding, and the glass case
big as Germany, knee-deep in human hair.

We grow quiet. We have crawled
into our eyes. There is nothing
but what we see. And at base bottom,
what's to see but the dredged-up bottom
of ourselves that belongs only to ourselves
and the moving tide of each other.
We crowd in to look. The eye is hungry—
a dog dragging its belly through streets,
sniffing out its own vomit, not getting enough:
the experiments, the ovens, and all their

tattooed histories fidgeting in smoke
that rose like bubbles in a fish tank
to dissipate in air. Fingers pluck
at our sleeves. Gold teeth hiss

in their case. What do they want of us,
we who can give nothing, reduced to nothing
but dumb pupils staring at evidence—
the starved and naked dead, the bulldozers,
the British soldier throwing up in his hand?
We press to the TV monitors, mob in,

fit our bodies together like multiple births
in the womb, wanting the heat of each other,
the terrible softness beneath clothes.
Excuse me, *Pardon*, and the knot of us
slips a little, loosens to make room.
In the smallest of voices, *Sorry* we say
as if, battered back to three again,
all we have is what Mother said was good.
Pinkie in a dike. Bandaid on a gusher.
But what else do we know to do

at the end of another century that retrospect
will narrow to a slit, if this Holocaust—
this boulder big as Everest—isn't big enough
to change the tide that ran through it?

Eyesore

To the west, Blacks.
To the east and southeast down the bend,
Whites. Between, the old couple—Monacan Indian,
perhaps the last—grazing their skinny cows,
hoeing their patch. The Mister once said, sure
he remembered me, but how *could* he, me coming
maybe five times in twenty years. But for me
he was fixture, made to order—baggy overalls,
grizzled cheek working a wad, Chevy pickup
up on blocks. One rusted geranium.

Now six years later I return—
country road, meadows, the old poplar
shimmying down one more October. My movie,
my pastoral, just waiting for me to walk my walk
and take my place. What didn't hold tight
until I came back? Even that brown dog,
trembling like a lover, showed up each day
to bark his heart out to my empty spot.

*   *   *

There are two kinds of not seeing—
when you can't or when you don't.
If you suffer from the latter, better depend
on shock, immense fallacies, mackerel
falling from the skies, or in this case
an empty yellow school bus careening, hell-
bent around the bend, headed for disaster or,
like a ghost on fire, fleeing one. A patch
spliced from a grade B movie to fill the hole
big as a bus left by what was missing.

The old man, gone—truck, barn,
house, the works. I tramp the empty yard,

trying to conjure up the groaning porch,
the ripped screen door, the annual geranium
anemic in its pot. But light glares.
The movie has let out early. And look.
Nothing but neatness and hush in a plot too flat
for these Virginia hills, and tread marks
running back and forth like a crazed eraser
with purple wildflowers scrambling over it fast
as if they knew what's buried there and would tell you
if they could take the time to stop.

SEYMOUR'S LAST RIDE

The night Flaming Dick & the Hot Rods
played the Shartlesville Fire Station Hall,
fog rolled over the Pennsylvania Turnpike.
So we pulled off, parked, unhooked the seats,
and having come straight from the funeral,
lay back for the night in our best dark clothes.

I wish I could say we weren't cold or stiff
or hadn't removed our shoes or that the fog
hadn't sealed us in so tight—the metaphor
too obvious, too A B C simple, suggesting
the old Choreographer had been reduced
to blocks and stringing beads. I swear

we were mock-ups in a case, coupled by proxy
to the limo we followed that afternoon
down Flatbush Avenue then east on the Belt—
a long thread of cars with no escort, only
the blunt needle of a hearse to pull us through
and deliver us up—a knot around a hole.

He lasted until the last hook of September,
the final days of red clover and ironweed,
when the cancer, sick of being chased
and stomped on like wildfires in a field,
retreated to his brain to feed and flourish,
sucking away in private. Strange, the ways

the earth's ten-thousand things see fit
to love us. Sidewalks lie back in bliss
to kiss our every step. Each pebble wants
inside your shoe. And see how every teaspoon
curves to hold your face, reluctant to lose it.
That night, semis mourned past us in fog

dragging their mud flaps. Noble ghosts
with blazing eyes. While beyond all hearing,
Flaming Dick and his Hot Rods revved up
the accordions for the last knot of dancers,
and *one & a two & a three,* squeezed out—
for sunshine and beaming water—a goodbye tune.

SUB ROSA

This year snow came late. The spring rains
early. Pressed in between, he failed.

That is, he couldn't hold on any longer
although they tried—fourteen drips, tubes
in as many orifices—or so it seemed.
Finally, the body wants its worm.

So he died. The thorn of who he was
or whether it had been enough, intact.
The closed door remained closed.
The seal unbroken. Maybe that's why
his family let it go on so long—two weeks
in that icy room holding his feet, his hands,
hoping for a sign, a twinge, a squeeze, anything
beyond what machines can count, what a doctor's
half-closed lids blink and refuse to deliver.

Words are what they wanted, what they
put him on the rack for—this husband,
father, this gruff man who never talked, who
ran his life the way he ran his grocery store,
lining up his days in rows of impenetrable tins,
face front, labeled, stamped.

But I remember the summers he could still
get out to tend his roses. How each Saturday
he'd choose one for the vase, crowning the bud
flaring into perfection. And how in June
when roses, so packed they jostle on stems the way
certain words of a poem will push, insisting
in the mouth, he'd line up four or five
on the kitchen counter where everyone could see—
one shameless beauty after another still throbbing

from the stem, like the sobs of a sentence
or the relief of betrayal
stammered by a heart's red tongue.

The Condensed Version

Simple as kindergarten—
she was not favored by the gods.
Don't hammer with chapter and verse.
Jesus never loved her.
Everyone else—liars, last-minute
confessors, cheats, bus-stop women
with glue-on nails. But not her.
Even the random one—
God of flukes and misunderstandings.
Old Poker Face. Lord of the Octopi—
eight possibilities and none of them right.

Periodically she'd run her empty cup
through the trash compactor
hoping for a stone to wear around her neck
to ease the one in her shoe.
She kept her nipple hairs plucked
and embraced the splash at the curb
as her due. In other words, she held on
as long as she could.

When she couldn't
she'd wander the back roads
looking for herself, then bring home
the pieces: a three-leaf clover, trash,
an earthworm who made the wrong turn
and ended up a squiggle—Rorschach
of the day she rummaged inside her wrist,
sure she'd found her old self at last
skipping in the ropes of her veins.

According to her husband
who dubbed her Saint after he found her
smelling like a goat in a sealed car,

she had filled up his life as the Amazon River
would an urn—well-wrought, of course,
and unbreakable.

THE GULF

to Madeline

Stephen Hawking tells us
we have four billion years left,
that's all. So when your call came,
no number, no message, no address,
I said good. After forty years
my begging bowl's too small
to hold all your change.

But don't imagine I forgot: the subway
running a vein down the west side
of Manhattan. And you and I,
three hours a day for four years,
rocking through morning rush hour—
French, anatomy, and bulging Achilles
careening on rails from the gut and burn
of Troy to the flats of Brooklyn.
Last stop, Flatbush and Nostrand,
and we like birds with human souls
pressed our breasts to our books
and bolted to class, running funny
the way girls did then, past the library,
across the quadrangle in kick-pleats
and little French heels with straps.
Even the trees were breathless.
Do you remember? those blooming cherries.

Here in Indiana, cold comes quick.
This morning, black clouds and wind
bullying April back to where it came from.
The sun struggling then giving up
as if the sky were a war going on forever—
before you and I rode the IRT
to school and disappeared,

blown apart or cut off like your hair.
Before Cain balled the first fist
and Achilles lay in the dirt
ripping at his face for his lost friend.

DUST

The lawn rolled back like a rug
in thick jellyrolls of sod
to be rolled back, flat again
as if nothing had happened.
What happened was dust, sealing
off one more job. I tell you,
there's no getting rid of it.
Beat your carpet back to thread.
Mop a floor, wash rocks. It waits—
pale and timid lullabyes

of fluff collecting themselves
in the dark, under your bed,
along baseboards. Bits of you,
yes, your skin, your hair, making
wee dollies with your name stored
in the sweeper bag, starting
another each time you throw
one out. Behind you, listen—
linty breath. There's no escape.
Fly to Rio, book a cruise.

Dust follows. *No no*, you say.
Tonight belongs to thunder,
to rain sloshing in, blinding
as car wash. Tomorrow's sun
promising a clean green world
bright as varnished lettuce. Oh?
Will it pass the white-glove test?
There's reason for the shiver
down the horse's rump. Slap it.
Watch the dust rise. See him run.

Preparatory Meditations

I begin with what to do at two.
Next chapter, three.
Then four and on into the late afternoon
of the Augean stables and the Jell-O
and the broth.

What happens today
may reveal the falling off the cliff
of tomorrow. I'll read no horoscopes.
Today shall be nothing
but the getting ready, for how
is it possible that this honey-duck,
this body, this *corpus delectable*,
would create its own betrayal? tuck me
in the nightly charm of a sleep
then slink about, fondling the corks
of flasks and secret vials?

A scummy pond says illness
with a green face.
My belly-skin looks peaches.

I know I know. Insides don't communicate.
My scars would tell,
but their tongues have been cut out.
And the only noise from the dark interior
is the intestine's babble—
the gut's galloping loop-
de-loop of gratitude—and the heart,
that case, that dementia,
that bloody verb,
that perpetual baby, bang bang banging
for its heat. Besides, how can

the body keep secrets from the brain?
Ah, but the brain—
that kiss in the head—tells no tales.
My hair's gone gray from straining
to listen through its roots.

They say in an airplane
if there's a crack in the glass,
you're sucked out and fall
like a shooting star, your last yell
pulling the zipper closed behind you.
Born through a slit
and out the same way. *Now, now,
none of that.* Remember, there are only
these instructions. These final pages
xeroxed from who-knows-what book.

TRIBUTE

Denise Levertov 1923-1997

December and we're driving home
to Arkansas, clouds coming in mean
and low, heavy with Christmas.
Overhead, the last strings of geese
limp south, gap and waver,
while inside each arthritic V
a tight formation of fly-boys,
next spring's Young Turks, memorize—
no nonsense—the way back home.

But this isn't about birds,
although when not daydreaming
out the window, I count the flybys
of tiny martins, multiple births
that swarm and circle the rice fields,
arcing up then dropping in unison
as if they'd been shocked
and swooned right out of the sky,
riding the currents like gnats
or floating plankton or the sardines
in a TV special that ball up
and sway about the seas, advertising.

Nor is this poem about fish
or any family of beast
that bonds, thinks, moves as one.
And it's not about Christmas
when we celebrate the pretense
that we do. It's about the poet
who died today and a radio announcer
who made of her life an assignment—
two sentences between commercials
then mangled her name. And how,

for a second, I swear I saw
all her poems come swooping down
in one last fall and gift, showing me
how none of that matters but the words
and how to set them soaring,
humming together in a sleeve of air
that suddenly explodes like a magic trick
or a star on the other side
of a galaxy—so far away by now,
everyone may not recognize her name.

VISITING ROBINSON

Since the time change
each day seems chopped off,
smashed like the edge of a Greek plate,
and I'm tempted to say darkness really is
gobbling up the sun, not slowly
but in big chomps. Gulping it down.
It is the time of the beast—reenactment
of an ancient war. The hunter
rules the skies. He's turned loose his dogs,
their eyes, hard and glittering.

Ferns pale to the color of celery,
brown out from the bottom, shrivel
and give up, disappear. Only the beech
keeps up appearances—gold medals and all.

Today I visited the studio of the poet,
stood where he stood, sat where he sat,
saw the same tree the same way
out the lead-paned window, ran my hand
over the plaque, wishing for a something,
an anything behind the familiar words:
I shall know more when I am dead.

I always loved that man's brass: the moody
brightness held up like an engraved shield
to a darkening sky. How he wore it—
old sot, old soldier, in the meaningless wars.

SUNDAY'S GIFT

from Van Gogh's Crows over the Wheat Field

Like Oedipus before him,
>> he stood where three roads meet—
>>> two bordered by green

one bare.
>> And wherever the grain
>>> heaved itself up between,

the black crows
>> rose, beating it down
>>> with their wings.

Giotto painted on his knees.
>> Delacroix wept.
>>> He studied the sky—

saw two places
>> the sun couldn't decide
>>> where to be. So he painted

blue covers over both
>> and nailed one shut
>>> with the bent iron bar

of a wing.
>> The other, he left—
>>> Little Orphan Annie eye

with a see-through lid.
>> A baby blue invitation
>>> reserved for a sun that never

came to any canvas painted in Auvers,
>> the last place he waited in
>>> and tried to live.

If you too stand
        where three roads meet,
                close enough

to bark at crows
        and chase the sun
                laying down its burning wall

brick by brick behind you,
        then remember him
                this Sun's day, for it was

always on a Sunday
        that he swallowed paint
                or drank the turpentine

from the jelly jar
        or cut off half his ear
                to gift wrap in a newspaper

for his whore.
        Mad Dog they called him,
                living in filth

and voices.
        A raging loony
                who could, until the end,

deliver the sun
        in a flower. Or crowned
                in a yellow kitchen chair.

Alice Friman, a New York City native, now lives in Milledgeville, Georgia. Her other books include *Zoo* (winner of the Ezra Pound Poetry Award), *Inverted Fire*, *Reporting from Corinth*, and four chapbooks. Her work has appeared in such publications as *Poetry, The Gettysburg Review, Shenandoah*, and *The Georgia Review*. She is professor emerita at the University of Indianapolis and presently teaches at Georgia College & State University, where she is the poetry editor of *Arts & Letters*. She lives with her husband, Bruce Gentry, editor of the *Flannery O'Connor Review*.